THE READING OF THE BIBLE

THIS BOOK IS PRODUCED IN COMPLETE
CONFORMITY WITH THE AUTHORIZED
ECONOMY STANDARDS

THE
READING OF THE BIBLE

As History, as Literature and as Religion

By

SIR FREDERIC KENYON

G.B.E., K.C.B., F.B.A., F.S.A.

LONDON
JOHN MURRAY, ALBEMARLE STREET, W.

First Edition . . . June 1944
Reprinted . . . . June 1944
Reprinted . . . February 1945

Made and Printed in Great Britain by Butler & Tanner Ltd., Frome and London

CONTENTS

CHAPTER I

PRINCIPLES OF BIBLE STUDY

BIBLE reading has been a notable characteristic of the English-speaking peoples from the Reformation to the end of the Victorian Age ; and its decline in the present century is a serious loss to the moral and cultural equipment of the nation to-day. Familiarity with the Bible has left an indelible mark on our literature and on our common speech : it has established moral and religious standards which cannot be shaken without grievous detriment. The Bible came to the people of England in their own language as a main weapon in the warfare which aimed at sweeping away the abuses that had befallen the Church in the Middle Ages. With the broadcast issue of the Great Bible in 1539 it became their common property ; and when the Authorised Version of 1611 set the final seal on the great work of William Tyndale and Miles Coverdale, they possessed the Bible in the incomparable dignity of beautiful language, and in a translation as faithful as the scholarship of the day admitted. Thenceforward it was the book of all classes. The Puritan movement carried it into the homes of the poorest people, to many of whom it was almost the only book with which they were acquainted. Its authority was unchallenged, and from its utterances there was no appeal. It was the one book which would be found in almost every house.

With the revival of religious life at the end of the eighteenth century the habit of Bible reading became intensified, and reached its height in the Victorian Age. Family prayers and the daily reading of portions of Scripture were common practices, and a general knowledge of the Bible could be presumed as part of the equipment, not only of the well-educated man but of the peasant and labourer. It was not a critical knowledge, for the age of criticism was then only dawning ; but it involved an acceptance of the Bible as an unchallangeable guide to right thinking and right living.

How then did this position come in fact to be challenged just when it was apparently at the height of its power ? The reason is to be found in the immense growth of knowledge which characterised the nineteenth century, and the dissemination of its results through the spread of education in all classes of the people. The Bible no longer stood alone. Its statements with regard to physical nature were challenged by the discoveries of natural science ; its history was brought into comparison with the newly discovered histories of the nations with which Palestine was in frequent contact. A critical spirit was characteristic of the period. It showed itself in dealing with the ancient classical literatures, and it inevitably attacked the traditional interpretation of the Bible. Learned scholars asked questions and raised doubts, which shallower men were eager to follow up in order to show their independence of mind. It became a sign of advanced thinking to question the authority of the Bible ; and criticisms which might be valid against its historical accuracy were converted into attacks on its moral authority. At the same time a vast half-educated class came into existence which could read and think and discuss, and was not prepared to accept the traditional beliefs of its predecessors. The authority of the Bible was shaken by scientific and archæological criticism, and the habit of reading it declined.

It is this situation which has to be met to-day by those who believe that it is not the essential value of the Bible, but only the validity of a particular view of it, that has been shaken. In the study of the Bible, as in the study of history, or of literature, or of natural science, the available evidence and the background change from age to age. The point of view differs ; the amount of illustrative material varies ; what one age finds it easy to believe, another age finds difficult or impossible. We have to recognise that we do not know everything, and that as knowledge grows, points of view must be adjusted. What was honestly believed in one age must with equal honesty be set aside in another. It is a part of the progressive education of humanity.

In this recognition of the progressive nature of our understanding of the Bible, there is no condemnation of those who in the past have offered different explanations or held (often with much obstinacy) different views. It has been just the same with the history of science. The Ptolemaic theory of the universe was the best attempt that ancient astronomers could make with the information available to them ; when Copernicus, confirmed by the telescope, produced a better explanation, men of science accepted it, often with some reluctance. It is no reflection on Newton that Einstein, with new data open to him through continued study and improved instruments, has been able to make modifications in his theory. The story of the theory of evolution offers an even closer parallel. Darwin's statement of it encountered fierce opposition at first, even among some scientists ; then it was generally accepted and regarded as fully established doctrine ; then further study led scientists to modifications of it, without affecting its general validity. It is therefore quite in accordance with the normal methods of our advance in knowledge, if from time to time our view of the teaching of the Bible, and of God's methods in the education of mankind therein revealed, should undergo modifications. The process of readjustment may sometimes be difficult, and new views must be tested by criticism ; but the process itself is natural, and new views should not be considered as necessarily hostile views. Readjustment does not involve the shaking of foundations.

Most of us are naturally wedded to the ideas in which we were brought up, and resent, sometimes bitterly, being asked to reconsider them.

On the other hand, those who are critically disposed, or who by temperament are rebellious, are inclined to reject " the traditions of the elders " with hostility and contempt. The extremists on the one side do not recognise that their views by no means always coincide with those of previous generations ; and the extremists on the other side often lack humility and do not recognise that their own opinions are not necessarily the last word in truth or wisdom, and may in time to come themselves have to be cast aside as outworn. Charity and modesty are useful ingredients in criticism, especially in dealing with beliefs which have become endeared by time, and which touch the inmost springs of action.

It is, however, mere matter of historical fact that methods of interpretation of the Bible have varied from time to time during the history of the Christian Church, and that the literalistic, uncritical views so prevalent in the Victorian Age have not always been held by the leaders of Christian thought. Origen, the father of Christian exegesis, explicitly affirmed that Scripture has a different force for different ages and different readers, according to their circumstances and capacities. He recognised also that the literal or historical nterpretation of the Old Testament could not always be accepted for the guidance of later ages. To meet this obvious difficulty he propounded the theory of a threefold interpretation of the Bible, literal, moral, and mystical ; and this theory had a far-reaching effect on the exegesis of the Middle Ages, so that in the hands of many commentators the allegorical interpretation far outweighs the literal. In the hands of such writers the interpretation of the Scriptures not infrequently becomes fantastic and grotesque, infinitely far from what we can believe to have been the intention of the authors.

On the other hand, the nineteenth century inherited the literalistic and piecemeal application of the Bible characteristic of the Puritans, to whom the English Bible came in the sixteenth and seventeenth centuries as a new light for their guidance direct from God. Since the Bible was the word of God, every part of it must be accepted as literally true ; errors in statements of fact were no less inadmissible than errors in moral teaching. If its authority was shaken in any one particular, it was shaken in all. Moreover, any words of the Bible might be wrested from their context and applied as universally valid in any sense which the words might seem to bear. Hence the common prevalence of " verse-hunting," in which the expressions of Scripture were interpreted without any reference to their original meaning or to the ordinary canons of criticism.

Underlying all these varieties of interpretation of the Scriptures were the theories of Inspiration held, explicitly or implicitly, by successive generations of Christian thought. Certain books—ultimately those included in the authoritative canons of the Old and New Testaments—were accepted by the Church as peculiarly " inspired," as prompted and filled by the Spirit of God for the guidance and instruction of mankind. From this the step was easy to the position that every word in these books was equally the direct word of God, in which the possibility of error was inadmissible. In the illuminated service-books of the Middle Ages an evangelist or prophet is frequently represented as writing with an angel whispering in his ear and dictating what he should write. The final step to the belief in the verbal inspiration of the particular form of the Scriptures known to the disputant was not difficult to the uncritical or the half-educated ; and on the other hand, those who could not shut their eyes to manifest errors and inconsistencies, or to moral standards no longer acceptable, were driven to theories of allegorical or mystical interpretation which more realistic ages found impossible and grotesque.

It is not easy to realise how recent is the acquisition of the knowledge which enables us to study the Bible in a truer perspective, and how modern is the growth of the critical spirit. Throughout the Middle Ages the Bible stood on a pedestal by itself, with no available standard of comparison. Even Latin literature was little known, and Greek much less. Other literatures were not known at all ; other religions were known only as the beliefs of the heathen, to be shunned as corruptions of the truth and the works of the devil. Even when the Renaissance had let in the light of Greek thought and had kindled the spirit of enquiry, it was long before this bore much fruit in either the search for knowledge or the application of scientific criticism. It was not until the nineteenth century that these two powerful engines of education came into full use. On the one hand, scholars attacked the prevalent opinions on the ancient literatures, whether classical or Biblical, with the acids of sceptical enquiry, which in turn called forth the defensive scholarship of those who held the traditional beliefs to be substantially sound ; and on the other, the archæologist set to work with his spade to reveal the monuments and records of the nations that immediately surrounded and were most closely associated with the Bible lands.

The first impact of this new knowledge and this new spirit of criticism was to shake confidence in the unchallengeable authority of Holy Writ. The second was to call forth a school of defensive criticism which applied the improved methods of scholarship to the sceptics' own views, and utilised in a conservative spirit the results of archæological research. What is now needed, and has been forthcoming, more or less, in many books of the last generation, to which this is only an addition, is a consideration of the results of this conflict of criticisms, and to see how far a new theory of inspiration emerges, which may reconcile the new knowledge and the new spirit of criticims with the authority of the Bible as a guide of life. It is an enquiry which must be conducted in the spirit of all modesty ; for it implies that knowledge is progressive, that we know more than our predecessors, but also that our successors will know more than we do ; that each generation must form its own synthesis by the application of its best powers of criticism to the knowledge available to it, and realising that, if it obtains for itself a light sufficient to walk by, its conclusions are but provisional, and that later generations will be able to walk in a brighter light, derived from a fuller knowledge.

At bottom, this is only to substitute the idea of a progressive revelation for that of an absolute revelation ; and a strong argument in its favour is its analogy with God's methods in His other dealings with mankind. It might have been His will to place man in a world where all was already perfect, where sin did not exist, where change, effort, progress were not required ; a world such as is imagined in Browning's poem " Rephan " :

There, all's at most—not more, not less ;
Nowhere deficiency nor excess.

No want—whatever should be, is now :
No growth—that's change, and change comes—how
To royalty born with crown on brow ?

Nothing begins—so needs to end :
Where fell it short at first ? Extend
Only the same, no change can mend !

None felt distaste when better and worse
Were uncontrastable : bless or curse
What—in that uniform universe ?

No hope, no fear : as to-day, shall be
To-morrow : advance or retreat need we
At our stand-still through eternity ?

All happy : needs must we so have been,
Since who could be otherwise ? All serene :
What dark was to banish, what light to screen ?

But into this peaceful, monotonous world comes the yearning
for change, for effort, for progress :

How did it come to pass there lurked
Somehow a seed of change that worked
Obscure in my heart till perfection irked ?

Till out of its peace at length grew strife—
Hopes, fears, loves, hates—obscurely rife—
My life grown a-tremble to turn your life ?

And so

You divine the test.
When the trouble grew in my pregnant breast,
A voice said, " So wouldst thou strive, not rest,

" Burn and not smoulder, win by worth,
Not rest content with a wealth that's dearth ?
Thou art past Rephan, thy place be Earth."

In the sphere of morality, it is clear that this world is a place
of trial, where cn man is placed the responsibility of using

the talents and powers with which he is gifted, where progress only comes with effort, and mistakes are possible. Why should it be otherwise with regard to the utilisation of the means placed at our disposal for our guidance in ascertaining and interpreting God's will ? He might have made a revelation to mankind which was absolute, imperative, leaving no room for variation or progress or differing interpretations, which mankind must follow without possibility of uncertainty or advance in standards, where the aborigine of Australia would be on the same level of moral apprehension and achievement as St. John or St. Francis. But it is evident that it is not so, that the need for effort, the possibility of progress, are no less necessary in the interpretation of His will than in the interpretation of His universe. In our reading of the book of nature we have progressed from the astronomers of Chaldæa, the philosophers of Ionia, through Ptolemy and Copernicus, Newton and Einstein ; and the end is not yet. Why should it be otherwise with our reading of the Bible ? Should we not expect, by analogy, to have to use our intellectual faculties for its interpretation, to advance in knowledge, to make progress in interpretation, without at any time derogating from its ultimate authority as a guide to life ? If the essence of the message remains unchanged, we may naturally look for human weaknesses in its transmission. " God, who commanded the light to shine out of darkness, hath shined in our hearts, to give the light of the knowledge of the glory of God in the face of Jesus Christ. *But we have this treasure in earthen vessels.*"

It thus seems to be in accordance with the general dispensation of the world in which we live that the revelation which we believe to be enshrined in the books of the Bible should bear the marks of the human channels through which it has come ; that its interpretation should be different in different ages ; that it should be differently understood, and therefore differently adapted to their own generations by Abraham, Moses, and Samuel, by Amos, Isaiah, and Ezekiel, by Paul and John, by Origen and Augustine, by Anselm and Aquinas, by Luther and Melanchthon, by the scholars and side is the inscription of Merenptah, discovered in 1896, which, among other triumphs of the king, records that " Israel is desolated, her seed is not ; Palestine has become a defenceless widow for Egypt " ; and the reference of this is obscure. But Egypt has produced, in the Tell el-Amarna Letters, a group of documents with direct information about Palestine. These are a group of tablets written in cuneiform script and the Babylonian language, found at Tell el-Amarna in Egypt in 1887, and comprising letters written by officials in Syria and Palestine to the kings Amenhotep III and IV, in the first half of the fourteenth century B.C. They are largely filled with pleas for assistance to deal with the inroads of invaders—Hittites, Amorites, and others—and representations of the disorder and ruin that are falling on the land. Appeals of this kind come from the governors of Byblus and Megiddo in the north, from Askalon, Gezer, and especially Jerusalem in the south ; and among the invading peoples in the south are mentioned the Habiru. It is tempting to equate this name at once with " Hebrew," and to see in these letters a picture of the invasion of Palestine by the children of Israel under Joshua. It may be so ; but the name Habiru is found in Babylonian and other documents in a much wider connotation, and at periods much earlier and later, and scholars are still much divided in opinion as to the date of the Exodus, some accepting the first half of the fourteenth century and others preferring the second half of the thirteenth. With further discoveries it may be hoped that these pieces in the puzzle will fall into their place ; at present one can only say that the light to be derived from Egyptian sources for the Old Testament history is small in quantity and doubtful in interpretation.

2. *Mesopotamia.* From Mesopotamia, on the other side of Palestine, we have many thousands of documents, from the third millennium B.C. downwards, written in cuneiform characters on clay tablets and cylinders. The earlier ones come from southern Mesopotamia or Babylonia, where the Sumerians had established a highly literate civilisation before the end of the fourth millennium. This has been brought to

light by excavations in the course of the last sixty years at such sites as Telloh (Lagash), Nippur, and Ur, which have yielded whole archives of documents, mainly of a business or commercial character, but including a notable number of literary texts. The most remarkable of these are the stories of the Creation and the Deluge ; but there are also lists of rulers, going back to the remotest mythical times, which show that here, as in Egypt, some system of annals was maintained. These no doubt provided the basis on which Berossus, a priest of Babylon in the third century B.C., formed his Greek history of Babylonia and Assyria, of which some scanty quotations have been handed down by Eusebius and Syncellus. Of direct historical narrative there is nothing ; but of materials for history there is a very valuable contribution in the Laws of Hammurabi, discovered in 1901 at Susa, whither the slab on which they are inscribed had evidently been carried as a trophy from Babylonia. The date of Hammurabi, king of Babylon, is now placed about 1792–50 B.C., somewhere, more or less, about the time of Abraham ; and though the similarity of these laws to those of the Pentateuch has often been exaggerated, they are unquestionably a proof of the existence of elaborately written legislation long before the time of Moses.

The records of the kingdom of Assyria, derived from the excavations of Layard, Rassam and others from 1843 onwards, principally on the sites of Nimrûd (Calah) and Kuyunjik (Nineveh), come much nearer to the character of direct history. The libraries of the temple of Nebo at Nineveh (from about 722 B.C.) and of Ashur-bani-pal (669–626 B.C.), besides containing religious texts (notably a later form of the Creation and Deluge story, incorporated in the legend of the hero Gilgamish), included also chronological lists of kings and of eponymous officials (known as *limmu*, who gave their names to the year, like archons at Athens and consuls at Rome), covering the period from the ninth to the seventh century. Far more detail, however, comes from the cylinders which it was customary to place in the foundation deposits of temples and palaces. These contain chronicles of the founders' reigns or of portions of them, and we have such cylinders of the Assyrian kings Tiglath-Pileser, Sargon, Sennacherib, Esarhaddon and Ashur-bani-pal ; also of the Babylonian sovereigns Nabopolassar, Nebuchadrezzar and Nabonidus, and the Persian Cyrus. Like the inscriptions of the kings of Egypt mentioned above, these are not objective history but self-laudations of particular sovereigns ; but they contain much historical detail, which (with a proper discount for the omission of unpleasant incidents) can be accepted. Some of it, moreover, directly touches on the history of the Hebrews ; notably the Black Obelisk of Shalmaneser, which records his defeat of Hazael, king of Syria, and the tribute paid by Jehu, king of Israel, and the cylinder in which Sennacherib describes his invasion of Judaea and the humiliation inflicted upon Hezekiah (but not the subsequent destruction of the Assyrian army).

Here, therefore, we get some cross-lights on Hebrew history, but not much ; and what we do get is not in the form of professional history. We have no continuous history of Babylonia or Assyria from native sources, and have no reason to suppose that any such existed except in the form of annalistic chronicles.

3. *The Hittites*. It is only since 1884 that the existence of the Hittites as a great empire in eastern Asia Minor has been made known by the discoveries and writings of Sayce and Wright, and at first the evidence consisted solely of sculptured monuments. But in 1906 a great record office of clay tablets was unearthed by Winckler at Boghaz-keui, from which something of its history has been recovered. Some of the tablets were in Babylonian script and language, which could be read at once ; others in cuneiform script but Hittite language, which have been slowly and laboriously deciphered by Hrozny, Forrer and others ; others again in Hittite hieroglyphs, which still await interpretation. These records established the identity of the Hittites, mentioned in the Old Testament, with the people referred to as Hatti in Assyrian documents and as Khita in Egyptian, and (in conjunction with the monuments) show that they occupied a large territory

with its capital in Cappadocia, and were a leading power in the Near East from the early part of the fourteenth century B.C. to about 1200, with a fluctuating authority over parts of Syria, and westward towards the coast of Asia Minor. Its power declined after the incursion of the mysterious " Peoples of the Sea," about 1194, but a loose Hittite confederacy continued to exist, with its centre at Carchemish, until its final suppression by Sargon in 717.

The Hittite documents include treaties with Egypt, and give us a number of place-names and names of kings ; but there is nothing of the nature of continuous historical narrative among them. They add to the proofs that documents providing material for history existed plentifully in the lands adjoining Palestine from a period before the entry of the Hebrews into that land ; but they offer no parallel to the historical looks of the Old Testament.

4. *The Canaanites.* The same may be said of the Canaanites of north Syria, of whom not only a record office but a royal library has been recovered by the French excavations at Ras Shamra (ancient Ugarit), near Alexandretta, from 1929 up to the outbreak of the present war. The date of these documents, most of which are written in a hitherto unknown alphabet of cuneiform characters, is in the first half of the fourteenth century, contemporary with the Tell el-Amarna letters and (if the earlier date for the Exodus be accepted) with the invasion of the Israelites under Joshua. Indeed, one of the texts, of a semi-historical character, describes the mission of Keret, king of the Sidonians, to oppose an invasion of the Negeb (southern Palestine) by a host of Terachites, whose name recalls that of the father of Abraham. But this narrative is plainly semi-mythical, and of direct history there is nothing. The great importance of the Ugarit library lies in its religious texts, which for the first time give us a picture of the Canaanite religion at the time of the Israelite invasion. They tell us of El, the supreme god, and of his son Baal, and in their worship we see the rival influence against which the servants of Jehovah were contending throughout the period of the kingdoms of Israel and Judah. They furnish us, as

14143

and sometimes inconsistent with itself. It is evidently a compilation of materials of varying characters and values strung together on an annalistic framework. It may owe something to " the book of the wars of Jehovah " (Num. xxi. 14), which may have included the invasion of Palestine as well as the previous fights with the Amorites and Midianites. Since the writer evidently had knowledge of the establishment of a kingdom of Israel (Judges xvii. 6 ; xviii. 1 ; xxi. 25), its date cannot be earlier than the age of Saul, and may more probably be later. For the Pentateuch, the analysis given above shows that what matters is not so much the date of its composition in its present form as the date of the materials of which it is composed. Until recently it was maintained by extreme critics that it could have rested on no documentary materials earlier than the period of the kings, because writing was not known earlier. Now it is clear, not only that writing was in common use many centuries before the date of David, but that elaborate legislation existed among the neighbouring peoples before the time of Moses. The books of the Pentateuch may therefore rest upon contemporary written records, and it is the task of criticism to discern and discuss them.

Thus, if we once accept the position that *we have this treasure in earthen vessels*, we can give an intelligible presentation of the character of the historical books of the Old Testament, regarded purely as history. The narratives of the Creation and Deluge and of the lives of the patriarchs may well have been handed down orally long before they were written down. In the households of Abraham, Isaac, and Jacob, and during the residence of the growing tribe in Egypt, it is not likely that there was any call for written records. But when we reach the age of Moses, we must take into account the general knowledge of writing and the compilation of codes of laws among the peoples of the Near East. The histories of the Hebrews may well have grown up much as the early chronicles of our own country, when one chronicler freely incorporated whole masses of his predecessors' works, and passed on the composite result to be utilised by his successors. So the authors of the histories which we know as J and E (see

p. 23), writing in the ninth or eighth century, would have utilised written materials (codes of laws, narratives, and the like) from the time of Moses downwards, and their works would then have been available for the historian or historians whom we know as P, who at the time of the Exile or Return set himself to compile the history of his people. Similarly, the author of the work which we know as the books of Samuel and Kings, writing after 560 B.C., had materials of earlier date, such as the lament of David for Saul and Jonathan, which he took from the book of Jasher, narratives of fact extracted from various annals ("the book of the acts of Solomon," "the chronicles of the kings of Judah," and the like), or the account of Sennacherib's campaign against Judah which is found in Isaiah xxxvi. and xxxvii.

The formulas which recur at the beginning and end of each reign (e.g. "In the twentieth year of Jeroboam king of Israel reigned Asa over Judah, and forty and one years reigned he in Jerusalem; and his mother's name was Maachah, the daughter of Abishalom. And Asa did that which was right in the sight of the Lord, as did David his father. . . . The rest of all the acts of Asa, and all his might, and all that he did, and the cities which he built, are they not written in the book of the chronicles of the kings of Judah? And Asa slept with his fathers, and was buried with his fathers in the city of David his father; and Jehoshaphat his son reigned in his stead") suggest that the compiler had before him an annalistic record of the successive reigns, to which he added fuller narratives when they were available. Thus the detailed account of the reign of Ahab with the acts of the prophets Elijah, Elisha, and Micaiah, is evidently derived from some non-official source, possibly from records kept by the corporation known as "the sons of the prophets."

Thus we have only to examine the books themselves to see that they are made up from materials of different dates and characters; and it will appear that we can apply to them the ordinary methods of literary and historical criticism without in the least affecting the moral teaching embodied in them, which is what gives them their value for us to-day.

(a) OLD TESTAMENT

The Old Testament, regarded as literature, is a collection of works of different ages, of varying character, and representing at least five distinct categories of literary form. It comprises (i) narrative works, which have been considered from the point of view of history in the preceding chapter, and now fall to be considered as literature ; (ii) poetry ; (iii) prophetical prose works ; (iv) sapiential works, i.e. the wisdom and proverbial literature ; (v) apocalyptic. These will be considered separately, in the light of the most recent knowledge and with reference to recent critical views, some of which may be of only relative and provisional value.

(i) *The Narrative Books*. These include the Octateuch (i.e. Genesis to Ruth), the books of Samuel, Kings, Chronicles, Ezra, Nehemiah, and Maccabees, with the romances of Tobit, Judith and Esther. Their dates, method of composition, and historical character have been discussed in the preceding chapter, and need not be re-examined here. Accepting the conclusions there indicated, they represent a body of narrative literature, the origins of which go back to the earliest ages, but the nucleus of which took form about the eighth century before Christ, and which for the most part had assumed its present form by the fifth century. For the purpose of comparison, which may enable us to appreciate better its special characteristics, we have, as in the last chapter, the literatures of Egypt and Mesopotamia on the one hand, and the literature of Greece on the other. The contrasts with these very different types of literature are illuminating.

From the literary point of view, Hebrew history is, for the most part, intermediate in style as in date between the annalistic methods of Egypt and Mesopotamia and the artistic handling of prose by the Greek writers. Some idea of their differences may be gathered from the following passages relating to the same subject, the invasion of Palestine by Sennacherib :

Cylinder of Sennacherib.

I drew nigh to Ekron and I slew the governors and princes who had transgressed, and I hung upon poles round about the city their dead bodies; the people of the city who had done wickedly and had committed offences I counted as spoil, but those who had not done these things and who were not taken in iniquity I pardoned. I brought their king Padi forth from Jerusalem and I stablished him upon the throne of dominion over them, and I laid tribute upon him. I then besieged Hezekiah of Judah, who had not submitted to my yoke, and I captured forty-six of his strong cities and fortresses and innumerable small cities which were round about them, with the battering of rams and the assault of engines and the attack of foot soldiers and by mines and breaches. I brought out therefrom 200,150 people, both small and great, male and female, and horses and mules and asses and camels and oxen, and innumerable sheep I counted as spoil. Himself like a caged bird I shut up within Jerusalem his royal city. I threw up mounds against him, and I took vengeance upon any man who came forth from his city. . . . The

2 Kings xviii. 11–16.

And the king of Assyria carried Israel away unto Assyria, and put them in Hulah and in Habor, on the river of Gozan, and in the cities of the Medes; because they obeyed not the voice of the Lord their God, but transgressed his covenant, even all that Moses the servant of the Lord commanded, and would not hear it nor do it.

Now in the fourteenth year of king Hezekiah did Sennacherib king of Assyria come up against all the fenced cities of Judah and took them. And Hezekiah, king of Judah, sent to the king of Assyria to Lachish, saying, I have offended; return from me; that which thou puttest upon me I will bear. And the king of Assyria appointed unto Hezekiah king of Judah 300 talents of silver and 30 talents of gold. And Hezekiah gave him all the silver that was found in the house of the Lord and in the treasures of the king's house. At that time did Hezekiah cut off the gold from the doors of the temple of the Lord and from the pillars which Hezekiah king of Judah had overlaid, and gave it to the king of Assyria. . . .

xix. 20. Then Isaiah the son of Amoz sent to Hezekiah, saying, Thus saith the Lord, the God of Israel, Whereas thou

Herodotus II, 141.

The next king, I was told, was a priest of Hephaestus, called Sethos. This monarch despised and neglected the warrior class of the Egyptians, as though he did not need their services. . . . Afterwards, therefore, when Sennacherib, king of the Arabians and Assyrians, marched his vast army into Egypt, the warriors one and all refused to come to his aid. On this the monarch greatly distressed, entered into the inner sanctuary, and before the image of the god bewailed the fate which impended over him. As he wept, he fell asleep, and dreamed that the god came and stood at his side, bidding him be of good cheer and go boldly forth to meet the Arabian host, which would do him no hurt, as he himself would send those who should help him. Sethos then, relying on the dream, collected such of the Egyptians as were willing to follow him, who were none of them warriors, but traders, artisans, and market people, and with these marched to Pelusium, which commands the entrance into Egypt, and there pitched his camp. As the two armies lay here opposite one another, there came in the night a multitude of field-mice, which devoured fear of the majesty of my sovereignty overwhelmed Hezekiah, and the Urbi and his trusty warriors, whom he had brought into his royal city of Jerusalem to protect it, deserted. And he despatched after me his messenger to my royal city Nineveh to pay tribute and to make submission with 30 talents of gold, 800 talents of silver, precious stones . . . and divers objects, a heavy treasure, together with his daughters and the women of his palace, and male and female musicians.

[tr. Budge]

hast prayed to me against Sennacherib, king of Assyria, I have heard thee. . . . He shall not come unto this city, nor shoot an arrow there, neither shall he come before it with shield, nor cast a mount against it. By the way that he came, by the same shall he return, and he shall not come unto this city, saith the Lord. For I will defend this city to save it, for mine own sake and for my servant David's sake. And it came to pass that night that the angel of the Lord went forth and smote in the camp of the Assyrians an hundred fourscore and five thousand : and when men arose early in the morning, behold, they were all dead corpses. So Sennacherib king of Assyria departed and went and returned and dwelt at Nineveh.

all the quivers and bowstrings of the enemy, and ate the thongs by which they managed their shields. Next morning they commenced their flight, and great multitudes fell, as they had no arms with which to defend themselves. There stands to this day in the temple of Hephaestus a stone statue of Sethos, with a mouse in his hand, and an inscription to this effect : "Look on me, and learn to reverence the gods."

[tr. G. Rawlinson]

The Babylonian chronicler shows little literary skill. He simply strings together a number of statements of fact, with no particular attention to effectiveness of phrase or rhetorical colouring. The Greek historian, on the other hand, has an easy narrative style, showing complete mastery of his language and ease in the formation of his sentences. Between these two the Hebrew writer shows less modulation of sentence-structure, with principal and subordinate clauses, than the Greek, but much more diversity than the Assyrian, and a much higher emotional colouring than either. He shows, for the first time in literary history, a real command of narrative, and in the message of Isaiah he reaches true eloquence, arising naturally from the deep stirring of his emotions, to which the Greek writer, whose emotions are not equally stirred, shows no parallel.

In literary structure and character the Hebrew history resembles the mediaeval chronicles of England rather than the work of the great Greek or of modern historians. In both the framework is annalistic, and the writer incorporates whole sections of previous chronicles instead of digesting their substance into a new narrative of his own. Thus, just as Roger of Hoveden incorporates a whole Durham chronicle, which itself was compounded from the works of Simeon of Durham, Henry of Huntingdon, Florence of Worcester and a Northumbrian chronicle, so the editor whom we know as P (see p. 24) incorporated large sections of J and E, who themselves had probably utilised previous writers, though we can no longer trace their borrowings in detail. Those who are familiar with our own chroniclers will find little difficulty in accepting, at any rate in general principle, the conclusions of modern critics with regard to the composition of the historical books of the Old Testament.

There are, however, some sections of the Hebrew histories which reach a far higher literary level than these annalistic chronicles, and which must have been derived from a different source. Such are the narratives of the life of David, the history of the reign of Ahab, the life of Elijah, and the invasion of Judah by Sennacherib. Here we find narrative skill of the very first order, notably in the conflict between Elijah and the priests of Baal on Mount Carmel, the appearance of Micaiah before Ahab and the death of the latter before Ramoth-Gilead, and the speech of Rabshakeh under the walls of Jerusalem. The source of these, as has already been suggested, may have been records kept by the " schools of the prophets," of the nature and activities of which we know little ; for it is significant that all these more detailed narratives, with the exception of the history of David, are associated with the activities of prophets—Elijah, Elisha, Micaiah, Isaiah. There is no reason to question the contemporary nature of these passages. The prophecies of Hosea, Amos, and Isaiah, which belong to the same period, amply prove the existence of

the ordinary reader to concern himself with these questions. He can take the Book of Psalms as a great anthology of Hebrew religious poetry, of the highest literary merit, and as expressions of thoughts and aspirations that are common to all humanity and that have lost no whit of their value in the course of the two thousand years and more since they were first composed.

The Book of Job is a continuous poem, with a preface (ch. i., ii.) and a postscript (xlii. 7–17) in prose. Of all the books of the Bible it is the most difficult to place, either in time or in locality. By the time of Ezekiel the name of Job was proverbially known as that of a traditional good man (Ezek. xiv. 14, etc.), but it does not follow that the poem then existed in its present form. The only indications of date are obtainable from its language and from the stage of development in monotheistic theology which it exhibits. All that can be said here is that the general tendency of scholars is to assign it to the late sixth or early fifth century before Christ. But in truth this does not matter. What we have here is a poem of permanent value, on a subject of permanent interest. Its subject is the problem of suffering, exemplified in the person of an Arab sheikh of exemplary character who is afflicted by overwhelming losses and tormenting disease. It is a problem as alive now as it was two thousand years ago. Is pain the punishment for sin ? If so, how are its inequalities to be explained ? If not, what is its justification, and how is its existence to be reconciled with the goodness and the omnipotence of God ? The poem sets out the problem in its various aspects, in the speeches of Job's friends and in Job's answers ; but it offers no final solution, for the magnificent passage with which it concludes (ch. xxxviii.–xlii.) is no more than an assertion of God's omnipotence and of man's inability to understand His ways. The only answer is submission and faith.

Scholars have doubted whether the Elihu episode (ch. xxxii.–xxxvii.) is an original part of the poem. It has a separate prose prologue (xxxii. 1–5) ; Job makes no answer to the arguments of Elihu, as he does to those of his three friends : and there is no reference to Elihu in either prologue or epilogue. It looks like an inserted attempt to provide the answer which the poem has failed to find. It can be cut out without affecting the structure of the poem.

An attempt has been made to assign to the poem a Babylonian origin. There is a Babylonian poem of about the seventh century which describes the sufferings of a virtuous man, who is eventually vindicated and restored to health. But the tone is different. It is not an assertion that suffering bears no necessary relation to sin, but rather an attempt to find out in what way the sufferer has offended his god. The problem of pain existed in Babylon as it exists to-day, and the Hebrew poet may have derived thence the suggestion of his subject ; but his treatment of it is different, and on a far higher level of religious thought and of literary performance. It is one of the great poems in the literature of the world.

The book that we know as " The Lamentations of Jeremiah " is not in the Hebrew Bible associated with the prophet. It stands apart, among the miscellaneous writings which form the third section of the Hebrew Canon. It is an elegy on the fall of Jerusalem, and its attribution to Jeremiah in the Greek Septuagint and the Hebrew Targum and Talmud is probably due to the passage in 2 Chronicles xxxv. 25, which says : " And Jeremiah lamented for Josiah : and all the singing men and singing women spake of Josiah in their lamentations, unto this day ; and they made them an ordinance in Israel ; and behold they are written in the lamentations." But the book is not a lamentation for Josiah, but for the destruction of Jerusalem, and it does not suggest the tone or language of the prophet. It is the work of an anonymous writer, written not in the first outburst of grief at the destruction of his country's capital, but somewhat later, when sorrow could be reduced to artificial literary form ; for it consists of four odes (ch. i.–iv.) in acrostic form, with lines divided into two parts, normally with three accents in the first and two in the second, followed by a fifth (ch. v.) which, though consisting of twenty-two lines, is not alphabetical and has lines of two equal portions, with three accents in each.

But though artificial in form, like a sonnet sequence, it is genuine in feeling, and expresses the real emotion of a lover of his city and nation.

The Song of Songs is unique among the books of the Old Testament, in that it has no religious character. It is a group of love poems, of much beauty but of secular character, and owes its inclusion in the Canon to the allegorical character imposed upon it, both by Hebrew and by Christian commentators. The Jewish interpreters regarded it as an allegory of the love of Wisdom or of God, while the Christians explained it as signifying the love of Christ for the Church. There is no authority for the attribution of the authorship to Solomon, and linguistic and other internal evidence points to the third century before Christ as its probable date.

(iii) *The Prophetical Books.* The institution of " prophecy " and the existence of a class of men (or occasionally women, Exodus xv. 20 ; Judges iv. 4 ; 2 Kings xxii. 14) known as " prophets " is one of the characteristic features of Hebrew history. The word " prophet " does not mean " one who foretells the future," but " one who speaks for " another, in this case for God. The prophets are those who claim to declare God's will, and so are the moral teachers and leaders of the people. Their origin is uncertain, and was probably gradual. Even if the description of Miriam and Deborah as " prophetesses " reflects the terminology of a later age, we find " companies of prophets " spoken of at the time of the anointing of Saul as king (1 Sam. x. 5, 10), the prophets Nathan and Gad in the time of David, Ahijah and the anonymous prophet of Bethel in the time of Jeroboam, Elijah and Elisha and Micaiah, and " the sons of the prophets " in the time of Ahab ; all which are evidence of the existence of this class of professional teachers before the days of the prophets whose works have come down to us in special books. These date from the early part of the eighth century and extend at least to the fifth century. The earliest group, that of the eighth century, includes Amos, Isaiah, Micah, Hosea. Then comes the period of the fall of the kingdom of Judah, from Josiah to the Captivity, including Nahum, Jeremiah.

Zephaniah and Habakkuk ; then the prophets of the Captivity and the Return, Second Isaiah, Ezekiel, Haggai, Zechariah, Malachi. Obadiah, Joel and Jonah are doubtful, Obadiah being probably of the sixth century, while the other two are now generally assigned to the early part of the fourth century. Daniel does not properly belong to the prophetical books at all, being partly narrative and partly apocalyptic. It is not included among the prophets in the Hebrew canon, but comes among the miscellaneous writings added at a later date ; and it is generally assigned to the second century.

Such is, in outline, the chronological framework of the prophetical books ; but the details admit of endless discussion. This arises naturally out of the nature of their composition and publication. They must not be thought of as orderly literary compositions, issued as complete works under the eyes of their respective authors. Rather they are collections of scattered utterances, put together at a later time, often in haphazard arrangement, and including pieces of uncertain authorship. The clearest instance of the inclusion of the works of more than one author under a single name is in the book of Isaiah. Here chapters i.–xxxv. are the work of the historical Isaiah, the great prophet contemporary with Hezekiah, composed of a number of prophecies uttered on different occasions, put together without regard to chronological sequence. Chapters xxxvi.–xxxix. contain a narrative extracted with slight modifications from the book of Kings, with the addition of the poetical Song of Hezekiah. Chapters xl.–lxvi. are the work of a different period and in a different literary style. They belong to the period after the destruction of Jerusalem, and are mainly devoted to encouraging the hopes of the restoration of Israel. Some scholars would further separate chapters lvi.–lxvi from xl.–lv., assigning the latter to the years 549–538 (the period of the rise of Cyrus), the former to the period after the return from the Captivity. How the work of this later writer or writers came to be attached to the collection of Isaiah's writings is unknown ; perhaps their high literary quality caused them to be assigned to the greatest of the known prophetical authors.

A similar combination of the work of at least two authors under a single name occurs in the book of Zechariah, where chapters ix.–xiv. are plainly not the work of the same writer as chapters i.–viii.

Another sign of the uncertainty attaching to the authorship of detached prophetical utterances is the occurrence of the same utterance in more than one collection. Thus Isaiah ii. 2–4 recurs in Micah iv. 1–3, and Isaiah xv. 2–7 and xvi. 6–11 appear again, with some variations of order, in Jeremiah xlviii. 34–43 and 29–33. There must have been much scattered literature of this kind—brief utterances of the prophet on some particular occasion, written down by himself or taken down by a hearer, and circulated in casual copies, often without a name attached to them, since everyone at the time knew who was the speaker, but eventually collected at a time when the author's name was forgotten. Some, on the other hand, would be longer and more deliberate compositions, such as the greater part of Amos, or the roll which Baruch wrote for Jeremiah and which probably formed the nucleus of the book which now bears that prophet's name. The marked difference in order between the Massoretic Hebrew text of Jeremiah and the Greek Septuagint probably reflects different arrangements of scattered prophecies once separately issued. But these details do not much concern the ordinary reader. It does not matter to him whether, for example, some parts of the book of Zechariah were actually the utterances of another prophet, whose name is now unknown ; his interest is in the intrinsic merit of these passages, as literature or as religious teaching. Some parts of all these books, which had meaning for the people to whom they were addressed, have little meaning for us to-day. Others, on the contrary, reach the highest splendour of literary expression, and embody religious truths of timeless value.

In style there is naturally much difference among these products of different authors and of different periods. Some books, or portions of books are in ordinary prose, e.g. Haggai, Jonah (except the hymn in ch. ii.), much of Jeremiah, the last section of Ezekiel (xl.–xlviii.), and parts of Isaiah, Hosea,

Amos and Zechariah. Others are definitely poems, with the same kind of metrical structure as we find in the Psalms and the other poetical books. Others again are written in a poetical prose style, in which the manner and vocabulary are poetical, but the rhythm is less definitely metrical.[1] There are also, naturally, great differences in emotional tension and in literary mastery of language, which can be felt as well in the English translation as in Hebrew.

It is as poetical prose of the highest order that the prophetical books make their literary appeal to the modern English reader. They reach their highest pitch in Isaiah and the Second Isaiah ; no reader can fail to be impressed by the magnificence and spiritual fervour of such passages as ch. v., vi., xi., xxv., xxvi., xxxv., or xl., li.–liii., lv., and indeed the whole of this prophecy ; or by the passionate earnestness of Jeremiah ; or by the pathos of Hosea xi.–xiv. ; or by the fiery emotion of Joel ; or by the spiritual exaltation of Amos. Quite apart from their religious significance, which is of the highest order, these are among the finest products of human literature, and the English reader, whether of the Authorised or of the Revised Version, can appreciate their quality to the full, and reckon them among the most precious treasures of his literary inheritance from the ancient world.

(iv) *The Proverbial Literature.* This, which is sometimes also called the sapiential literature, since it is largely devoted to the praise of Wisdom, is a characteristic branch of Hebrew literature, though one which it shares with other Oriental peoples. It is represented by the books of Proverbs and Ecclesiastes in the canonical Old Testament, and by Wisdom and Ecclesiasticus in the Apocrypha. The last of these has a known author, Jesus the son of Sirach. The others have the name of Solomon connected with them, and in view of the tradition recorded in 1 Kings iv. 30–2 there is no reason to doubt that this manner of writing, though not invented,

---

[1] In the R.V. only the hymns in Jonah and Habakkuk are printed as verse ; but the reader can feel for himself the poetical structure of much of the other prophets. Oesterley and Robinson (*Introduction to the Books of the Old Testament*, 1934, p. 224) class Joel, Obadiah, Micah, Nahum, Habakkuk, Zephaniah and Malachi as wholly poetic.

was firmly planted in Hebrew literature by him. The testimony is explicit and significant : " Solomon's wisdom excelled the wisdom of all the children of the east, and all the wisdom of Egypt. For he was wiser than all men ; than Ethan the Ezrahite, and Heman, and Calcol, and Darda, the sons of Mahol ; and his fame was in all the nations round about. And he spake three thousand proverbs, and his songs were a thousand and five." This is clear evidence of the existence of a recognised wisdom-literature, both to the east of Palestine, that is in Mesopotamia, and in Egypt. Whether the unknown " wise men " named in this connection were earlier or later than Solomon, it is impossible to say, though the natural presumption would be that they were earlier. That there was a recognised class or category of " wise men " appears from Proverbs xxii. 17 and xxiv. 23 ; but Solomon was regarded as pre-eminent in it, and it is quite unjustifiable scepticism to ignore this solid and definite tradition. On the other hand, it is quite certain, from the internal evidence of the books themselves, as will be set out in the analysis of them given below, that the greater part of them has no claim to Solomonic authorship, and it is quite impossible to say what particular passages can be assigned to him.

Wisdom literature is of great antiquity in the East. It may be defined as the literature of moral admonition, ranging from precepts of the commonest worldly wisdom to a high level of religious exhortation. It appears in Egypt as the earliest class of literature that has come down to us. The oldest extant Egyptian book is the Prisse Papyrus, which contains the Teaching of Kagemna and the Teaching of Ptah-hetep. These works were composed in the time of the IIIrd and Vth Dynasties respectively, i.e. about 3100–2850 B.C., and the papyrus itself belongs to about the end of the third millennium ; but the moral precepts contained in them were still being copied under the XVIIIth and XIXth Dynasties, only some two or three centuries before the time of Solomon. Here are a few samples from the Teaching of Ptah-hetep : [1]

[1] From *The Teaching of Amen-em-apt*, by E. A. W. Budge (1924).

Magnify not thy heart because of thy knowledge, and fill not thy heart with the thought about it because thou hast knowledge.

Follow thy heart's desire as long as thou livest, and do not more than is ordered.

Weary not thyself concerning the affairs of the day, nor be anxious overmuch about thy house and estate.

Be not avaricious when a division of property is made, and be not greedy, and what is thy due shall come to thee.

Satisfy thy servants whom thou trustest with thy possessions, so that they may feel as if they had been rewarded by God.

Repeat not the words spoken by a man who is furiously angry; hearken not to him; they are the outpouring of a heated mind.

If thou art strong, make respect for thyself to spread with understanding and with gentleness of speech.

Command not except when thou canst guide; abuse brings a man to calamity.

It is a bad thing to set oneself in opposition to the man who is appointed chief. A man lives as long as he displays gentleness and patience.

Let thy face shine with cheerfulness as long as thou livest. . . . Do not let any man approach thee and find thee with a gloomy face.

The admonitions of Ptah-hetep are addressed to his son; they are the maxims of worldly prudence, the observance of which is calculated to secure his advancement in life. Many of them refer to the behaviour to be adopted towards superiors. More general in character, and with more moral intention, is the Teaching of Amen-em-apt, or Amen-em-ope, a later work, which shows resemblances, and even coincidences, with the book of Proverbs such as to suggest a direct connection between them. Here are some examples : [1]

Amen-em-ope	*Proverbs (R.V.)*
Give thine ear and hear what I say, And apply thine heart to apprehend.	Incline thine ear and hear the words of the wise, And apply thine heart unto my knowledge.

[1] Taken from the article by W. O. E. Oesterley in *The Legacy of Egypt* (1942), pp. 246–8. Oesterley dates the Egyptian work to about the middle of the eighth century ; Budge puts it much earlier, in the first half of the XVIIIth Dynasty, i.e. about the end of the sixteenth century.

ing through the crust of traditional exegesis which had established itself during the Middle Ages. The Reformation was largely based on the dissemination of knowledge of the Bible through vernacular translations, such as those of Luther in Germany and Wyclif and Tyndale in our own land ; and this led to a more intense study and realistic interpretation of the Scriptures. Luther uncompromisingly denounced allegory, and maintained the right of private judgement, with adherence to the literal sense and consideration of times and circumstances. Allegorical interpretations, which, like cobwebs, had obscured the natural meaning, were swept away finally, and misinterpretations tended to the opposite extreme, the uncritical application of texts without reference to their context or, in some cases, their true meaning. The Bible was regarded as a quarry from which passages could be drawn for controversial purposes. In our own country this was very conspicuously evident during the period of Puritan ascendancy. Since the publication of Coverdale's Great Bible in 1539, and still more when the Geneva version of 1557–60 brought the Bible into the homes as well as the churches, the Bible had been taken to the heart of the English people. Its text was well known and widely used. The combatant tone of the Old Testament was especially congenial to the militant spirit of Puritanism, and the soldiers of Cromwell and the Covenant delighted in references to the sword of the Lord against Midian, the slaughter of the Amalekites, and Samuel's execution of Agag. Expressions suitable to a primitive age and savage manners were applied to a later age which should have known better, and the New Testament doctrine of love was obscured by the ruthless ethics of early Hebrew intolerance.

This age of violence wore itself out at last, and was succeeded by the somewhat colourless tolerance of the eighteenth century ; but the Wesleyan missions of the latter half of that century and the Evangelical and Anglo-Catholic revivals of the nineteenth led to a renewed and intenser study of the Bible, with the emphasis rather on the New Testament than on the Old. Most of this was entirely to the good ; its defect was, however, the same in principle as before, namely the application of texts without reference to their context or true meaning, as though any words found in the Authorised Version of the Bible must be regarded as authoritative in any connection to which they were verbally applicable. The main danger of this frame of mind lay in its production of a temper which regarded any criticism of the Bible as a denial of its authority ; which treated as enemies of the faith those who tried to assimilate the results of modern literary criticism or discoveries of historical facts ; and which, by defending the indefensible, imperilled the safety of that which was truly precious. Thus, when the progress of knowledge and humanity made it impossible to accept as permanently applicable the universality of the Flood or the glorification of indiscriminate massacres of enemies, there were (and are) those who said that to question the complete validity of any part of the Bible was to question the authority of the whole, and whose acceptance of the doctrine of the New Testament was shaken by any doubt thrown on the historical accuracy or the universal moral applicability of parts of the Old.

It is against this temper, which (in colloquial phrase) would throw out the baby with the bath-water, that is set the alternative method of approach, which, by laying stress on the principle of progressive revelation, would retain the full moral and religious value of the Bible while rescuing it from an impossible position of conflict with historical and scientific fact. The determination of what is fact, and what is merely insecure assertions of fact, remains open ; the assertions of subversive critics are no more immune than the assertions of fundamentalists ; but the discussion of them can be conducted without the feeling that the essential truths of faith and religion are imperilled, and without the intolerant and uncharitable tone of controversy which sometimes rises from that feeling.

In the principle of progressive revelation, as has been said already, there is nothing new. Augustine himself admitted it, though he rarely uses it. It is inherent in the progress from the Old Testament to the New. No Christian would mind of the people of Israel, and no more majestic assertion of it is to be found in all literature. The revelation of the New Testament in no way supersedes this declaration of the power and majesty of God, though it adds the manifestation of Him as the God of love.

Together with the early prophets, the book of Job may be mentioned. Its date is doubtful, but its representation of the Almighty is similar. The universal and unquestionable power of God is its constant theme. It is to Him that Job appeals, acknowledging Him as the controller of all that happens, and demanding to know why all this suffering has fallen on him. God " is wise in heart and mighty in strength . . . which alone stretcheth out the heavens and treadeth upon the waves of the sea ; which maketh the Bear, Orion and the Pleiades, and the chambers of the south " (ix. 4–9). " Who knoweth not in all these that the hand of the Lord hath wrought this ? In whose hand is the soul of every living thing, and the breath of all mankind " (xii. 9, 10, etc.) ? And in the magnificent finale of the book the Lord Himself proclaims His power over all creation, as the answer to the complaints and criticisms of His creatures, for whom His ways are past finding out. God is the universal source of being, omnipotent and without rival. Man can only abhor himself, and repent in dust and ashes.

The prophets of the end of the kingdom and of the Captivity and the Return reach no higher standard than the prophets of the eighth century, and strike no new note. Jeremiah and Ezekiel are concerned mainly with denouncing the backsliding and idolatrous worships of the people, and in foretelling their captivity, with only the consoling hope of the eventual (but not speedy) return of a remnant. The assumption of the power of Jehovah over all peoples is common to them all. Like Isaiah, Jeremiah and Ezekiel pronounced judgement in the name of the Lord on Moab and Edom and Ammon, on Tyre and Egypt and Babylon ; and Nahum and Jonah declare the doom of Nineveh. Jeremiah proclaims explicitly the supremacy of Jehovah : " The Lord is the true God, he is the living God, and an everlasting king ; at his wrath the earth trembleth, and the nations are not able to abide his indignation. Thus shall ye say unto them, The gods that have not made the heavens and the earth, these shall perish from the earth and from under the heavens. He hath made the earth by his power, he hath established the world by his wisdom, and by his understanding hath he stretched out the heavens " (x. 10–12) ; " Behold, I am the Lord, the God of all flesh " (xxxii. 27).

A higher note than the assertion of power and the denunciation of vengeance is struck by the Second Isaiah : " The glory of the Lord shall be revealed, and all flesh shall see it together ; for the mouth of the Lord has spoken it. . . . Behold, the nations are as a drop of a bucket, and are counted as the small dust of the balance ; behold, he taketh up the isles as a very little thing. . . . All the nations are as nothing before him ; they are counted to him less than nothing and vanity " (xl. 5, 15, 17). " Thus saith God the Lord, he that created the heavens, and stretched them forth, he that spread abroad the earth and that which cometh out of it, he that giveth breath unto the people upon it, and spirit to them that walk therein ; I the Lord have called thee in righteousness, and will hold thine hand, and will keep thee and give thee for a covenant of the people, for a light of the Gentiles ; to open the blind eyes, to bring out the prisoners from the dungeon, and them that sit in darkness out of the prison house " (xlii. 5–7). " It is too light a thing that thou shouldest be my servant to raise up the tribes of Jacob, and to restore the preserved of Israel ; I will also give thee for a light to the Gentiles, that my salvation may be unto the end of the earth " (xlix. 6). The canon of the prophets ends with the conception of a God who is the loving father as well as the omnipotent ruler and judge, and with the promise of the coming of the Sun of Righteousness with healing in his wings (Malachi iv. 2).

The more intimate and personal side of Hebrew religion is to be found in the Psalms ; but the uncertainty of the date of many of them makes it impossible to trace in them the development of religious thought. A considerable number of them are odes in celebration of the power and glory of God (e.g. xix., lxv.–lxviii., cxliv.–cl.) ; but the commonest theme of all is the appeal to that power for help, either generally or specifically against enemies. Many of them couple the appeal for help with denunciations of the wicked oppressors, and demands for their punishment. Several (e.g. cxv.–cxviii., cxxiv., cxxvi., cxxix., cxxxv., cxxxvi.) are hymns of gratitude for mercies received. There is ample recognition of God's goodness (xvi.–xviii., xl., xlii., liii., cvii.) ; but only a few (vi., xxii., xxxii., xxxix., li.) express at all strongly a personal sense of sin. The fatherhood and loving kindness of God are recognised in such Psalms as viii., lxxxi., lxxxix., ciii. There are also a few notable pictures of the character of the upright man (i., iv., v. xv., xxiv., ci., cxii.). The beauty of virtue and of good conduct towards others is amply acknowledged ; but the dominant theme is the greatness of God, the creator and ruler of the world, the defender of His chosen people, whose merit is to obey His Law, and who look to him for very present help in trouble. " O worship the Lord in the beauty of holiness ; let the whole earth stand in awe of Him " is a cry that sums up much of the feeling of this collection of poems—the power and holiness of God on the one hand, the worship due to Him from man on the other, and the beauty of this relation.

(b) New Testament

There is no need to dwell long on the period that lies between the later Prophets and the books of the New Testament. It is a period of great importance in the development of Jewish religious thought, and it prepares the background against which our Lord's life was lived and Christianity was first preached. But it has left little mark on the Bible, with which we are here concerned. Its main features are (1) the Wisdom literature, and (2) the apocalyptic literature. Both of these are represented in the Apocrypha of our Bible, the former in the books of Wisdom and Ecclesiasticus, the latter in 2 Esdras. In neither does religious doctrine or philosophy rise to a higher level than had been already reached by the prophets ; but the conception of Wisdom, as expressed in these books, went some distance in preparing the way for the doctrine of the Word of God, as we find it in St. John. The apocalyptic literature, on the other hand, expresses the general unsettlement of mind, the longing for a saviour and a judge who will avenge the cause of the righteous, the hopes of a coming kingdom of righteousness, which were characteristic of the period ; but it lies almost wholly outside the limits of our Bible, even of the Apocrypha.

In the New Testament we reach the climax of our religion, the revelation of God in Jesus Christ. It would be quite beyond the scope of this book to attempt even a summary of that revelation. While the main theme of the Old Testament is the Power of God, that of the New Testament is His Love. This is what we find in the narratives of our Lord's life and the letters of His followers, which compose the New Testament. All that can be done here is to suggest a method of approach to them.

It is necessary to realise how informal and incomplete our records are ; and it may be of some use to recall their chronological relationship. The earliest documents are the Epistles of St. Paul—letters written by him to various Christian communities as occasion arose. None of them purports to be an ordered exposition of the Christian faith. Only once, in the earlier part of the epistle to the Romans, does he undertake a formal inquiry into a particular point, the relation between the Law and the Gospel. For the rest, they are ἀγωνίσματα εἰς τὸ παραχρῆμα, occasional utterances called forth by the particular circumstances of the community which he was addressing. His knowledge of our Lord's life and teachings must be picked up from scattered passages and individual references. That St. Paul had access to the general body of narrative then available, we know from his own words : " I delivered unto you first of all that which also I received, how that Christ died for our sins according to the scriptures, and that he was buried, and that he hath been raised on the third day according to the scriptures," etc. (1 Cor. xv. 3, 4). This corresponds exactly with the reports in Acts of the first preachings of St. Peter after Pentecost. All the emphasis was on the Crucifixion and the Resurrection ; and to this were evidently added narratives of His life and teaching, such as we find in the Synoptic Gospels. St. Paul gives an example of these in his narrative of the institution of the Lord's Supper (1 Cor. xi. 23 ff.) ; but he makes no systematic use of them. Rather he assumes in those to whom he writes a general knowledge of the historical facts underlying Christianity and the main substance of its teaching ; and he comments only on such particular subjects as serve his immediate purpose.

The general tradition, which at first passed from mouth to mouth orally, and eventually took form in the Synoptic Gospels, no doubt represents the substance of the teaching and preaching of the apostles and their followers, addressed to the newly-converted and those whom they wished to convert. It comprises miracles and other incidents which would attract listeners, and the simple teaching based upon them, and instruction given by our Lord in language which could be understood without much difficulty. That discourses more profound and difficult were also delivered to the inner circle of disciples, there is no reason to doubt. In particular we are told that He did so during the forty days between the Resurrection and the Ascension. How far they all understood it at the time may be doubtful ; but they had the teaching given to them to meditate on, and were promised the guidance of the Holy Spirit to help them to understand and develop it. It is this that may explain the special character of the Fourth Gospel. As was argued above, the increased (in fact, now definitive) proof of its first-century date makes it increasingly difficult to refuse the traditional ascription of it to St. John. He was one of the inner circle of the disciples from the first ; and he, as the Gospel shows, must have had special gifts of spiritual discernment. He had a good memory, as the wealth of small details in his narrative shows (see above, p. 60) ; and he had had a long life in which to turn over in his mind what he had heard. That his expression of it would take the colour of his own style (and it will be observed that his epistles are very similar in style to the Gospel) is natural enough ; there is a parallel in Plato's representation of his master Socrates. But the substance may well be that of the more intimate discourses of Jesus. The teaching of the Lord had to reach the world through many minds. There were the more pedestrian minds of those who passed on the stories and the sayings which they had heard ; there was the mind of St. Peter, strong, straightforward, passionately in earnest ; there was the cultivated scholar's mind in St. Paul, fired with an ardent zeal for the conversion of souls ; and there was the gentle, loving, meditative mind of the Beloved Apostle. But all these can be facets of the same mind of the one Master, interpreting to the world different aspects and details of the same teaching.

Nor need the reader be distressed by the fact that centuries of discussion were necessary before the Christian faith received its final formularisation. The assertion of a faith prompts questions and criticisms. To these criticisms answers have to be found, and these answers are again criticised until formulas are found which define beliefs hitherto held without much definition.

Formularisation is the protective bark of the tree, necessary because the truth has enemies, or mistaken friends, whose errors must be warded off. It is natural that the acute minds of the East should have had many questions to put to so strange a doctrine as that of the Christians. It is natural that divergent interpretations should have been offered, and the great leaders of Christian thought should have had to fight hard for the interpretation which they regarded as the true one. The controversies had their worldly side, sometimes not very edifying ; but the Christian is within his rights in believing that the Holy Spirit guided the course of events to the climax of the Nicene Creed.

There are those who denounce " dogma," and say that they can only believe an undogmatic religion. They are apparently unconscious that they are talking nonsense. " Dogma " means formulated belief. It is just as much " dogma " to say " I believe in a God," or indeed to say " I do not believe in a God," as it is to say " I believe in the

14143

INDEX

b. BIBLICAL PASSAGES CITED

(Quotations are according to the Revised Version)